The State of Local Government in Jamaica: A Portrait of the Municipal Corporations

Copyright © 2024 Paul W. Ivey, PhD
All relevant rights reserved.

ISBN: 9798880017713

****#****

Contents

******

About the Author

****

Dr. Paul W. Ivey is a cerebralist and griot-scholar, who is also an active and engaged Jamaican citizen, griot, public adult educator, historian, and the author of 17 books (so far) that are trellised upon robust research and solid scholarship. His books are crafted to animate and augment readers' minds and are available in e-book and paperback formats on the Internet.

****

About 'IveyBooks'

****

Books written by Dr. Paul W. Ivey are called 'IveyBooks'. They all share the following common 'signature features' of being data-rich and well-researched because in writing them he deploys the 'scholarship of integration', which is the scholarly methodology that involves the acquisition, selection, distillation, synthesizing, and contextualizing of information from many sources to create new insights and understandings for readers. It is this methodology that gives rise to the value proposition of 'IveyBooks': the guarantee that they will enhance readers' minds.

****

Other Books by Paul W. Ivey

****

"I pour a lot of intellectual energy into my books ... 'IveyBooks' are well-researched and data-rich ... and the ideas and thoughts are communicated clearly with lively and lovely prose." ~ Paul W. Ivey

****

JAMAICA: Paradise and Paradox, Volume 1

JAMAICA: Paradise and Paradox, Volume 2

JAMAICA: Paradise and Paradox, Volume 3

It All Began With The May Rains: An Introvert's Remarkable Journey (Autobiography)

My Daughter and Me: Parenting a Polymath

Silent River

The Matriarch: The Life & Legacy of Edith "Pearl' Ivey

The Golden Boy

Toxic Masculinity: Disordered Models of Manhood in Jamaica

****

Citadels of Incompetence

****

Jamaica's Local Government Authorities, the Municipal Corporations, are individually and collectively citadels of incompetence. Their incompetence is exceeded only by their obliviousness to their incompetence and the lack of capacity for shame on the part of their membership and leadership.

Like a corpse's odour, so awful is the manifestation of the incompetence of the Municipal Corporations athwart Jamaica that you cannot escape its pervasiveness.

Shame is a complex and powerful emotion characterized by feelings of embarrassment - the collective leadership of Jamaica's Municipal Corporations is devoid of this emotion.

Today, disorder is evident everywhere and is commonly associated with, and is a blot on, the Jamaican brand. This disorder is largely the result of the gross incompetence of the Municipal Corporations.

As a credible academic, I have curated in this book copious and incontrovertible evidence to support my characterization of Municipal Corporations as 'citadels of incompetence'.

I will start by describing the state of affairs in Jamaica's capital city and some other major towns in Jamaica. They, and the ones I have not included, all share one common feature: disorder and chaos set in permanence.

Kingston

"A squalid violent horror."

As evidence of the endemic incompetence of the Municipal Corporations, I will start with Kingston – Jamaica's storied, 'bipolar' and bustling capital that, in 2016, based on its rich musical heritage and other cultural offerings was named by UNESCO as a "Creative City of Music."

Now, a nation's capital should be safe, clean, orderly, and a place of national pride. Alas, not so Kingston – it is depressingly dirty, disorderly, decaying, grimy, and wreathed with signs of poverty and palpable mismanagement that ought to be cause for the indictment of the responsible persons in the Kingston & St. Andrew Municipal Corporation for gross negligence and dereliction of duty.

I can't imagine how these people collect their salaries without feeling guilty.

They are bereft of the capacity for shame. They are shameless co-conspirators to chaos! You see, there is a social value to shame.

Social research has shown that shame is not always a negative thing. It can lead to positive social results.

However, the shame-deficit in the Kingston & St Andrew Municipal Corporation (KSAMC), and others, is remarkable – remarkable in the sense that a train wreck is remarkable.

Consider this: "In the capital city (Kingston), public order is rapidly disappearing, leaving a growing criminal element to rob, maim, and murder with impunity. As one travels around the city, the deterioration is palpable. Just visit Half-Way-Tree any night when the police are not out in numbers, and observe the mayhem created as the 'loaders' for public transport and street vendors take charge." [Source: Arnold Bertram, 'Take Warning,' The Gleaner, August 16, 2019]

There is more distressing commentary from citizen Winston Barrett: "Let us, for a moment, use the cities of Kingston and Montego Bay as examples. These cities represent the core of our economic activities in tourism, commerce, and manufacturing, contributing a large percentage of our gross domestic product. Yet, we have allowed a morass of violence and lawlessness to fester, with our streets littered with garbage and illegal and unsightly vending in all areas, including, believe it or not, outside the gates of the Canadian and Japanese ambassador's residences in the so-called Golden Triangle." [Source: The Gleaner, March 16, 2020]

Then there is this confession: "Jamaica has been suffering from bad planning for too long!" confessed Senator Pearnel Charles, Jnr. when he was delivering the keynote address at the 2nd Conference on Sustainable Development, held at the University of Technology, Jamaica, on November 7, 2019.

I strongly disagree with Senator Charles because Jamaica has some wonderful plans on paper. The problem is the poor implementation that is often compounded by corruption and other negative factors.

There is a 'school of thought', grounded in the racist ideology that fuelled slavery and colonialism, that, concerning Blacks, "A class more totally unfit to govern (themselves) does not exist upon the face of the earth."

This point of view is, of course, vile racist rubbish. But it pains me to say that, in Jamaica, Municipal Corporations, by their manifest incompetence, flaccid impotence, and shamelessness, seem determined to give credence to the obscene, racist trope.

Globally, elected officials, policymakers, and city planners are actively working to create environmentally friendly, safe, and resilient communities, neighbourhoods, and cities for their citizens.

Alas, this is not the case in Jamaica. The authorities in the municipal corporations have obviously abdicated their responsibilities. And evidence of this abdication is everywhere seen.

On March 4, 1996, Patrick O. Stanigar, an architect, delivered the 11th Alexander Bustamante Memorial Lecture, at the Jamaica Conference Centre. These are some of the points he made, "Cities are reflections of cultures. And always reflective of a people's character. Kingston, as our city, is our reflection. Jamaica's tragedy is Kingston's. We have allowed an essentially beautiful little city to develop in a squalid, violent horror. Kingston is our reflection, and it is sick. Are we going to watch ourselves die in the mirror?"

The answer is a depressing and sad 'yes' despite the JLP breezily stating in its 2016 Manifesto that, "We will revitalise and rebuild our town centres and cities ... We will start with the redevelopment of the Kingston waterfront and market district."

More than three decades after Patrick Stanigar's lament and three years after the JLP's Manifesto was published, on March 14, 2019, Gary 'Butch' Hendrickson, the chairman and CEO of Continental Bakery Limited, was the Keynote Speaker at the Opening Ceremony of the University of Technology, Jamaica's annual Research, Technology, and Innovation Day. I was present. Hendrickson cited an example of the "silliness" that he believes is illustrative of the impotence of the **Kingston and St. Andrew Municipal Corporation** – not fixing little problems like the pothole-riddled intersection of Knutsford Boulevard and Trinidad Terrace in New Kingston – a major intersection in what is Kingston's swanky business centre.

"There is a puddle of water, and five weeks after they fix the road, there is (again) a puddle of water with potholes because nobody thought that when you wash the sidewalks of New Kingston, we need a drain. Now, do we really have to continue to do things like that?"

Hendrickson also bluntly criticised systemic deficiencies that weaken good governance. He alluded to a lack of visionary town planning as a major hurdle to efficient traffic management. He also said that municipal authorities did not understand that a comprehensive organisation of society, including facilitating access to accommodation for low-income residents, was a core responsibility of the State.

'All I Want for Christmas is ... Sidewalks!' was the title of an article published in **The Gleaner** on December 22, 2019, by Rachelle McFarlane, Senior Lecturer at the University of Technology, Jamaica, in which she lamented navigating the 'obstacle course' of Kingston's sidewalk-less roads with her toddler in a stroller: "Santa, all I want for Christmas are stroller/wheelchair accessible and properly paved sidewalks. pedestrians are being forced into the path of motorised vehicles since no provision has been made for them. Even to the untrained eye, we have driven through residential zones and commercial zones, and we have seen ramshackle, overgrown, converted to extensions of stalls, blocked by utility poles/panels, or absent sidewalks. So, this simply forces the pedestrians, young and old, able and disabled, fast and slow, to walk on the paved surface, aka the road. It is baffling that the authorities responsible for managing our road network can approve rehabilitation works and even brand-new projects that exclude the creation of sidewalks for pedestrians. Gordon House and responsible agencies, let us really look at Vision 2030 in creating sustainable cities and make prudent decisions. Most of us travel overseas and we take for granted that citizens and visitors are outside walking on sidewalks; children riding their bikes on sidewalks; people standing at the bus stop on sidewalks; wheelchairs, strollers, walking canes, you name it, all of them are on the sidewalks. This is not a feature ONLY for developed countries; it is a feature of governments that see the importance of protecting its citizens."

Given the current awful state of the City of Kingston, I was stunned when I read an article in The Jamaica Observer by Jean Lowrie-Chin on November 11, 2019, about an event where the Mayor of Kingston was present. "We enjoyed the positivity of Mayor

Senator Delroy Williams, who described his beloved City of Kingston as the 'Pearl of the Caribbean,'" Lowrie-Chin wrote.

I was shocked on reading what Lowrie-Chin wrote – could it be that 'His Worship' Mayor Williams is satisfied with the "sick, squalid, and violent horror" Patrick Stanigar described? This tells me that Mayor Williams is proud of his monk-like devotion to mediocrity.

Half-Way-Tree (HWT) Square has become one of the quintessential locus of chaos and lawlessness in Jamaica!

Spanish Town

"Dirty and chacka, chacka."

I am compelled to mention that Spanish Town, Jamaica's former capital city, like Kingston, is, today, also a "sick, squalid, and violent horror" despite the JLP stating in its 2016 Manifesto that, "We will revitalise and rebuild our town centres and cities..."

Besides, it is noteworthy that the United Nation's Sustainable Goal #11 is 'Sustainable Cities and Communities.'

Spanish Town, the former capital of Jamaica, is worthy of comment: "Spanish Town was the Spanish and British capital of Jamaica from 1534 until 1872.

The town is home to numerous memorials and one of the oldest Anglican churches outside England. Architecturally, Spanish Town remains a national treasure. Near the town`s entrance stands the oldest iron bridge of its kind in the Western Hemisphere. Cast in England, it was erected in 1801 at the cost of £4,000. On the eastern side of the Square, where the Assembly used to be, is now housed the offices of the **St. Catherine Parish Council (renamed Municipal Corporation)**. The original House of Assembly was built in 1762. On the south side of the square stand the burned remains of the former Courthouse, built in 1819, the victim of a 1986 fire. It is believed that on this site once stood the Spanish Church of the White Cross, said to have been connected by an underground passage to a monastery on nearby Monk Street. Also, nearby on Barracks Street is the remains of the military barracks erected in 1791 to house both soldiers and officers. A large underground passage has been discovered there, although its origin and purpose remain elusive. East of the square on Red Church Street stands the Anglican Cathedral on the site of the Spanish Chapel of the Red Cross, which was destroyed by Cromwell`s soldiers. The first Anglican

Church building was destroyed by a hurricane in 1712 and rebuilt in 1714. In 1843 it was named the Cathedral of the Jamaican Diocese of the Anglican Church. A mixture of many different architectural styles, including medieval, the Cathedral is shaped like a cross and includes several monuments by John Bacon. The floor is graced with marble headstone memorials to prominent British colonists that date as far back as the 1700s. Next to the Cathedral, now known as the St. Catherine Parish Church, is the St. Catherine District Prison. The history of Spanish Town lives on in the remnants of the old buildings that harken back to days gone and in the street names that mark it as a microcosm of the island`s overall history." [Sources: Black, C. (1960). 'Spanish Town - The Old Capital'; Sherlock & Bennett (1998) 'The Story of the Jamaican People'; Rebecca Tortello, 'The Story of Spanish Town' – 'Pieces of the Past' (The Gleaner, May 19, 2003); Wikipedia]

The foregoing is the history of Spanish Town.

But, Reader, this is the sorry state of Spanish Town today, presided over by another shame-deficient and mediocrity-worshipping municipal corporation – the **St. Catherine Municipal Corporation**: "The town has degenerated over time and the urban fabric of

Spanish Town like many other towns in Jamaica is currently in a deplorable state. Words like crime and violence, evil, dirty, and ghetto have been used to characterize the once prosperous town. A feeling of fear and hopelessness is ever-present when one navigates through the zinc fence and shack-filled town, where squatter settlements and street-side vendors seem to be at the forefront in every direction. The streets are unsightly with uncovered drains containing black. Squalid water and unfriendly sidewalks throughout the Town Centre. Further compounding the thought that this place is a forgotten town is evident in low levels of public or private developments or investment, while crime and violence have stained the name of Spanish Town." [Source: 'Citizens' Vision for Urban Regeneration: Spanish Town through the Eyes of the People,' Adrian Hewarston Hall, Master of Architecture Thesis (supervised by L. Mark Taylor and Dr. Elizabeth Pigou-Dennis, University of Technology, Jamaica, 2018)]

The excerpt immediately above from Mr. Hewarston Hall's thesis speaks for itself, and I need not add anything else.

But I will.

I have traversed the town centre and several satellite communities of Spanish Town and have seen with my own two eyes their absolutely deplorable state.

Chacka, chacka sums up the state of Spanish Town.

One of the most obvious eyesores is the highly trafficked roundabout at Old Harbour Road at the end of the Spanish Town by-pass – it is overgrown with bushes and terribly unsightly and obstructs the visibility of motorists using the roundabout. This level of continuous dereliction of duties is simply mind-boggling to me.

There's more. "A section of the Spanish Town bus park in St. Catherine has been transformed into a mini version of the Riverton City dump as the authorities are left to grapple with a garbage collection and disposal nightmare that has morphed into an unsightly health hazard," read a report in The Gleaner of December 18, 2019.

On February 8, 2024, I visited the Spanish Town Centre. Later that day I posted on my Facebook page that it could be summed up in one word: "Chacka-chacka."

My post provoked several comments, which I now share:

- "Dutty & stink .. recently a schoolmate and I were reminiscing on how we were able to walk through the Nº 5 cemetery and read the headstones as you know lots of history is in cemeteries. Also, we could walk along the train line from St. John's Road to the Train Station. Now it's a city with ramshackle lean-to the whole length of the way. Spanish Town is a DISGRACE."
- "Does not even begin to describe…it would take tomes."
- "Nasty. Dutty. Stink. Nuff criminal a lurk every weh. Chakka chakka. Scary. Only LOJ Mall or Bashco mi go mainly. Dat town fi mi is….go in, get an item, cut (leave)."
- "And so much history that is being left to crumble into decay. It is mind-boggling and borders on 'criminal negligence'."
- "Not to mention Young Street and other areas with murky water, sometimes have to step in to avoid being hit by vehicles."
- "Successive governments have failed the people. Spanish Town my old stomping

ground especially on Fridays to get a taxi or minibus to go home from school. I have fond memories of walking to the area of the courthouse where there were some old buildings. Also walking through the market. There was nothing to fear except fear itself.”

- “It's true the bad roads and sewage are a big turn-off.”

Linstead

“Chaos set in permanence”

I made the following post on my Facebook page on December 18, 2021, about Linstead, **'Chaos Set in Permanence - My Drive through Linstead earlier this week'**: “Growing up in Ewarton, St. Catherine, Linstead was the closest 'big Town' to me. People from Ewarton went to Linstead to conduct important personal business like seeing their doctor, banking, and 'taking out' furniture on hire purchase. Of course, there was the famous Linstead Market - immortalised in the song 'Carry mi ackee go a Linstead Market' - where many Ewartonites would sell stuff as vendors (e.g., my paternal grandmother), and purchase items as customers. As with most 'Towns', Linstead had its share of congestion - people, their stuff, buildings, and cars in competition for space. As a teenager/young adult, I visited Linstead countless times. I left Ewarton in 1981 to pursue educational opportunities and have lived elsewhere since. Of course, with my parents and family members still living there, I've visited my hometown over the years. Before the construction of the Linstead by-pass road, I drove through Linstead on my 'home visits'. But after the by-pass was built, I rarely drove through Linstead anymore, visiting only if I had a particular reason to go there. So, I have not been to Linstead in many years. But I had to go there on Thursday of this week. A friend and I travelled from Kingston. We took the North-South Highway (I am not calling it that other forced name) off the Mandela Highway and then eventually pulled off at the Linstead exit. As we headed toward Vanity Fair, we were welcomed by the unkept verges, the uneven surface of the main road, and the general haphazardness of everything. But it was when we entered the town centre that we were enveloped by totalising chaos. By this time, I was driving at a snail's pace, surrounded by a sea of people doing their own thing as they pleased, without the slightest hint of orderliness. This was complemented by the din from loader men, vendors seeking customers, and impatient motorists honking their cars' horns. My friend kept asking me if I was sure I wasn't lost and was off the correct main thoroughfare through the town. We took the better part of an hour to get through the town centre, having taken about 20 minutes from Kingston to get to the Linstead exit on the North-South Highway. I wonder what Linstead is like on Saturdays. The Town of Linstead is a symbol of the perennial dereliction of duty and impotence of both central and local governmental authorities and the police to maintain order in public spaces in Jamaica - from Morant Bay in the east to Negril in the west. This entrenches a mindset of 'anything goes' among the population and chaos (chacka, chacka-ness) becomes normalised - set in permanence! Perhaps I need to get over myself, but I cannot resign myself, as a citizen, to accept this level of mediocrity. Until order is restored in public spaces athwart Jamaica, we will never get a handle on crime in this country. This is about psychology. The **'Broken Window'** theory is apt. But whenever references to the transformation of Singapore by Lee Kwan Yew are mentioned, nuff Jamaicans get up in dem feelings misunderstanding that the point is not advocacy for his methods, but that transformation of a country is possible - within the context of its culture and history - with transformational leadership. Jamaica's current Prime Minister – Andrew Holness - was born on July 22, 1972, making him 50 years old - a young man – at the time this book had been published. Does he intend to transform Jamaica? I mean, where can we look for effective leadership of our country, that is manifested in, for example, the maintenance of order in public spaces such as the Town of Linstead?

A year after my Facebook post about the disgraceful state of Linstead, in December 2023, Television Jamaica (TVJ) carried a two-part feature on the town. On the back of the TVJ feature, I reposted my post and it generated several comments that I will share now:

- "Yes, real dirty."
- "And the behaviour of the people in the town is just a reflection of the grime ...real disgusting."
- "Linstead is like a small Riverton City Dump on any given day Sunday to Sunday."
- "The town needs cleaning every street and corner it is a disgrace i went there today and garbage all over."
- "Yes, yes, yes!!!"

- "I took one of my friends from the USA with me and my cousin that lives in the UK to Jamaica on vacation and I was so embarrassed to see that little slip of road between the Rose Duncan Park and the NCB bank, it's unbelievable!"
- "Is civic pride even a thing anymore?"
- "Why can't the relevant authorities maintain order in our town centres and other public spaces in Jamaica? Why?"

Perhaps I should not have been surprised about the chaos set in permanence in Linsted given that, like Spanish Town, it is under the purview of the emphatically incompetent and truly hapless St. Catherine Municipal Corporation.

Mandeville

Cecil Charlton served as a Councillor of the then Manchester Parish Council for 38 years, 15 of which as mayor of Mandeville.

During his tenure, Mandeville was regarded as the 'cleanest town in Jamaica'. Paying tribute to Charlton when he died in 2013, then-Custos Rotulorum of Manchester, Sally Porteous, who also served the parish council for many years, said Charlton not only cleaned up the town of Mandeville but "ruled it with an iron fist...for no one would dare drop anything on the ground when he was mayor".

Then-Mayor Brenda Ramsay of Mandeville said the parish council owes a "debt of gratitude" to this man, who changed the way the council operated. "This little man with the big voice and a whole lot of confidence... was impatient of those who gave excuses for why things could not be done, he did not tolerate slackness...".

Today, sadly, Mandeville has 'evolved' to be as disordered and chaotic as all other major towns in Jamaica.

Other Major Towns

The following major towns in Jamaica are disordered and chaotic: Annotto Bay, Brown's Town, St. Ann's Bay, Port Maria, Port Antonio Morant Bay, May Pen, Santa Cruz, and Savannah-la-Mar.

****

Mandate of the Ministry of Local Government

****

I visited the website of the Ministry of Local Government and Community Development to ascertain the mandate of this ministry vis-a-vis the Municipal Corporations.

This is what the website says: "The Ministry of Local Government and Community Development acts as the agent of local development. This covers the areas of:

- Development planning;
- Minor water supplies;
- Municipal parks & beautification;
- Markets;
- Parochial road maintenance;
- Poor relief;
- Street lighting;
- Solid waste management;
- Fire services;
- Disaster preparedness and emergency management;
- Local government amenities i.e., abattoirs, pounds, and cemeteries."

The website continued: "Local government reform was added when a Reform Unit was established in 1994 guided by a policy paper written a year earlier as well as extensive discussions on the issues over the years."

Functions of Municipal Corporations

Concerning the roles and functions of Municipal Corporations (previously called 'Parish Councils'), this is what the website of the Ministry of Local Government and Community Development says: "Local Authorities are empowered to make by-laws, regulations and rules for the good governance of the parishes over which they have jurisdiction." The website mentions several specific functions, but I want to highlight these:

1. Developing, managing, and maintaining infrastructure and public facilities such as parochial roads, water supplies, drains and gullies, parks, recreational centres, markets, abattoirs, pounds, cemeteries, transportation centres, public sanitary conveniences, and public beaches.
2. Provision of local services such as poor relief, public cleansing, public health, and street lighting.

3. Regulation powers with respect to building and planning approvals and development control, licensing of trades and businesses, street parking, and control of public vending.
4. Spearhead plans and initiatives for the orderly, balanced, and sustainable development of the parish as a whole, and major towns in particular, and the boosting of economic activity and local wealth creation within the parish.

Functions of the Mayor

Under Jamaica's Local Government Act, the Mayor plays several important roles and functions within the local government system. These functions may include:

1. **Chairing Municipal Corporation Meetings**: The Mayor presides over meetings of the Municipal Corporation, ensuring that proceedings are conducted according to proper procedures and that decisions are made in the best interest of the municipality.
2. **Representing the Municipality:** The Mayor serves as the official representative of the municipality in various capacities, including

interactions with other levels of government, community organizations, and the public.

3. **Advocacy and Lobbying:** The Mayor advocates for the needs and interests of the municipality, lobbying for resources, policies, and support from higher levels of government and other stakeholders.

4. **Budgetary Oversight:** The Mayor typically plays a role in the budgetary process, working with council members and municipal staff to develop and approve budgets that allocate resources effectively to meet the municipality's needs.

5. **Policy Development:** The Mayor may be involved in the development and implementation of municipal policies, working with council members, staff, and stakeholders to address local issues and achieve community goals.

6. **Community Engagement:** The Mayor engages with the community to understand concerns, gather feedback, and promote civic participation in local decision-making processes.

7. **Ceremonial Duties:** The Mayor often participates in ceremonial events and functions, representing the municipality and fostering a sense of pride and identity among residents.

8. **Public Relations:** The Mayor serves as a spokesperson for the municipality, communicating with the media and the public to provide information, address concerns, and promote transparency and accountability in local government.

9. **Conflict Resolution**: The Mayor may play a role in resolving conflicts or disputes within the municipality, working to find equitable solutions and maintain harmony within the community.

Revealingly, a Nationwide News Network/Blue Dot poll conducted in early 2024, found that an overwhelming majority of respondents did to know what were the functions of the Municipal Corporations!

Worryingly, respondents in the 18-24 age group were least likely to know what were the responsibilities of the Corporations.

Every one of the Municipal Corporations has been unmitigated failures in all the above functions for which they have responsibility.

Bar none.

The pathetic performance of the Municipal Corporations has lured me to the conclusion that their leaders are devoid of 'shame receptors'.

On November 15, 2018, I attended a forum at the University of Technology, Jamaica titled **'Building the Way Forward: The Impact of Urbanization on Rural Communities in Jamaica – Examining Public Infrastructure, Land Reform and Sustainable Livelihood'**.

Notably, the forum was organised by graduate students in the Faculty of the Built Environment.

Panelists at the forum included the head of School and Land Management; Dean and former Dean, Programme Director, Faculty of the Built Environment; the Mayor of Kingston; the Member of Parliament, St. Andrew Eastern; the Director, of Squatter Management Unit, Ministry of Economic Growth and Job Creation; and City Engineer from the Kingston and St. Andrew Municipal Corporation (KSAMC).

The Forum confirmed two things to me: that Jamaica is not a failed state but is a state that is failing in many ways, and that, as devices, Municipal Corporations are singularly and collectively impotent contributors to chaos and disorder in Jamaica!

Spurned by the Electorate

Based on the collective pathetic track-record of the municipal corporations, the Jamaican electorate, as measured by voter turnout for municipal elections, spurns them. The majority of eligible voters have spurned the Local Government elections. Many don't even know their local Councillors. A poll conducted between January 19 and February 6, 2024, by 'Blue Dot' for Nationwide News Network found that "When it comes to knowing who their local candidate is, 70 percent of voters in Kingston and St. Andrew say they had no clue. In St. James, 68 percent of voters do not know their candidate. Sixty-two percent of voters in St. Catherine and Clarendon say they do not know their candidate. Only St. Mary, Portland, and St. Elizabeth had a majority of voters indicating they knew their candidates."

In addition, a RJRGLEANER Communications Group-commissioned poll by Don Anderson found that "Forty per cent of Jamaicans have ranked the island's municipal corporations as poor or very poor managers of the nation's business at the local level, with another 40 percent saying their performance was just average." A mere seven percent of respondents gave the parish councils a "very good" rating, whereas 13 percent said they were "good". The polls took place between February 2 and 7, shortly after the February 26, 2024, date for the local government elections was announced by the Minister of Local Government. Using a sample size of 1,010 registered voters across the 14 parishes, citizens were asked several questions about their local representatives over the last seven years.

The top five reasons responders gave for giving the municipal corporations a failing grade, 60 percent of responders said their elected local representatives (Councillors) were missing in action; 57 percent said poor road construction; 26 percent said lack of access to water; 23 per cent said no jobs were being created; and 10 per cent said lack of green spaces.

Robert Stephens, co-chair of civil society group the Advocates Network, was not surprised by the poll findings: "I'm not surprised at all. I think what really needs to happen is that there needs to be far more focus on the performance of local representatives, and it is really up to all of us to demand more in terms of representation," Stephens told **The Sunday Gleaner**.

The municipal corporations have been assessed by the electorate and found to be seriously wanting - they are terminally ineffective!

From **The Gleaner** on December 20, 2023: "In all municipal elections so far this century, voter turnouts have trailed the preceding parliamentary election by over 20 percentage points, with the 22.45 percentage points in 2016 being the narrowest. The widest differential during the period was 29.9 percent turnout in December 2007, compared against the national parliamentary elections the previous September, when 61.48 percent of the electorate voted."

In a poll conducted between November 24 and December 7, 2023, by the Don Anderson-led Market Research Services Ltd., 38 percent of Jamaicans said they will vote in municipal elections due by February 2024.

What accounts for this marginal increased interest in the municipal elections? Per **The Gleaner**: "The pollsters observed, there is additional interest in the forthcoming municipal elections because they are more than two years overdue, having been delayed twice."

The 2024 Election

Local Government Elections were last held on November 28, 2016. Local elections are to be held every four years.

However, undemocratically, the elections were postponed for various reasons by the sitting JLP government. The last postponement was based on the patently spurious reason that the government "didn't have the money." The decision was raw political expediency of the kind many Jamaicans did not expect from Prime Minister Holness.

For the record, it must be stated that the People's National Party has also postponed the Local Government Elections when it held the reins of government. This just underscores my view, and that of other Jamaicans, that Local Government is really a fiction' – central government run things!

Besides, both major political parties have used the local government elections as a kind of gauge of their support in national polls.

In fact, the opposition PNP has dubbed the 2024 elections as a "referendum on the performance of the JLP." "The whole of Jamaica is treating this like a general election. It's like a preliminary general. The excitement is at a different level to what LGE [local government elections] normally encounter. The people are dying to send a signal to this Government that they want to get rid of them ...," said PNP President Mark Golding. [Source: The Gleaner]

And the governing JLP has been campaigning (without announcing the date, I might add) as if it were a general election.

Dr. Orville Taylor of the UWI agrees that the elections were a de facto referendum: "It is disingenuous for anyone to suggest that these are not very important elections. The governing Jamaica Labour Party (JLP) has control over almost all of the parish councils nationally. Therefore, in many ways, this is a referendum, a test not only of the validity of the polls, conducted by Don Anderson and others."

I agree with **The Gleaner's** position that was published in its editorial on February 11, 2024, that "The interest of democracy insists on greater certainty on the timing of both the municipal and national polls" and that "The parties must declare their positions on the issue. In fact, it should be among the questions explicitly posed to the political leaders and/or their surrogates at any debate on local government, including a demand for precisely how they would guarantee fixed-date elections and timetable for getting done."

The Gleaner continued "The surest guarantee is by anchoring the requirement in the Constitution and tied to a similar arrangement for national parliamentary elections. That way, both elections could be held at the same time, saving taxpayers billions of dollars by not having to spend on two elections within a year of each other. Indeed, a fixed, unadjustable cycle for elections, except in the most dire of circumstances, ought to appeal to, and be embraced by, Prime Minister Holness. While in opposition he pledged, if he won the government, to implement such a system for parliamentary elections. "Within our first 100 days of government, we will start the legislative process to fix the date for general elections in Jamaica," Mr. Holness told a campaign rally a fortnight before his party's victory. 'This will bring greater certainty to the political process...' It is more than seven years since Mr Holness made that pledge. Little has happened since then to move the process forward."

The Local Government Elections were finally announced to be held on February 26, 2024, to elect Councillors for the 228 divisions nationally – 499 candidates were nominated.

Councillors represent constituents within the divisions comprising a municipal corporation. The importance of local government derives from the fact that it represents the closet point of contact between the people and the public apparatus that provides essential basic services.

In the lead-up to the election, public affairs commentators lamented that, instead of focussing on issues relevant to local governance, the campaign focussed on national issues, dwarfing and drowning out local issues in the process.

"If one looks at the issues being put forward by both parties, the majority are of a national nature. There's very little parochialism in the electioneering contest," Lloyd B. Smith, a former deputy Speaker of the House of Representatives, told **The Gleaner**.

Smith said if one were not fully aware that it was a local election that has been scheduled to take place a week and a half from now, it could be concluded that the country is in the throes of a general election. Along a similar line, Dr. Paul Ashley noted that advertisements from the two main political parties have not centred on candidates participating in the election. "The prime minister has indicated that this is a serious election, and he is busy campaigning not for particular candidates - we have not seen them. We have not heard anything other than I am a candidate and I will win." [Source: The Gleaner]

For his part, former Member of Parliament Ronald Thwaites, writing in **The Gleaner** on January 22, 2024, described the election as "Semi-useless because little or nothing is being credibly advanced to improve basic services by the municipalities. Instead, the main purpose is to use the poll to gauge the political temperature in preparation for the general election. Garbage is inadequately collected everywhere and obtaining streetlights is to be considered the height of a Councillor's eight-year term. Everything that should have been routinely delivered is being brazenly promised again."

Labelling the election as a "Contest without a purpose", Thwaites continued, "It becomes clear what we should have known already, that local authorities have no autonomy. There is no evidence that people fare better at the municipal level if one or the other party wears the mayor's necklace. Not even lip service is paid to the principle of subsidiarity – an essential foundation of caring democratic governance. I predict that nuff money will have to run in the next few weeks to ensure even a half-decent voter turnout. Our taxation dollar, forcibly taken from all of us, is going to be shelled out to some of us to bribe us to participate in an electoral process which most of us know will have very little if any positive effect on our lives. And the candidates with access to the most money will prevail."

The Jamaica Debates Commission organised two debates between selected representatives of the Jamaica Labour Party and the People's National Party.

On 'X' (formerly Twitter), someone posted "I want to hear how you (the candidates for a given division) are going to take charge of the parish council – cleaning up our town, regular time-tabled de-bushing, maintenance of public spaces, parks ... basically make the place look like it has an owner."

The poster was basically calling for a debate between the candidates at the local level. I most certainly agree with this point of view!

Another poster had a different view: "A debate on the Local Government Election won't solve the problems we have with the system. A public education awareness campaign would be more useful. Why debate something very few of us know about?"

Below are my five questions that, if I had the opportunity, I would ask both sides in the debate:

1. Some citizens say the concept of 'local government' is fictional because the central government controls them ...What are your views on how Municipal Corporations may be truly empowered and given real autonomy?

2. What are your views regarding the Constitutional Reform Committee being asked to include among reforms, removal of the discretionary ministerial power to make local policy and dissolve local government authorities?

3. In the 2016 LGE, the voter turnout was a mere 30.6%. How can citizen participation in local governance arrangements be strengthened, and what specific initiatives would you implement if you win?

4. Judged by the low voter turnout, citizens have lost confidence in the effectiveness of the Municipal Corporations ... how can Municipal Corporations up

their game and gain the confidence and respect of citizens?

5. Should the Parochial Revenue Fund be abolished and Municipal Corporations be allowed to keep the monies they collect from property tax and tax on motor vehicles, fees on building permits, etc. and spend it locally as they see fit? Can you please share your views on this matter?

****

Examples of Failures

Reader, I cite the following examples in support of my conclusion:

Commercialisation of Residential Communities

The Municipal Corporations have singularly and collectively presided over the lack of enforcement of zoning laws across the length and breadth of Jamaica. Many formerly 'residential communities' have been overrun with commercial buildings and activities.

On March 18, 2015, **The Sunday Gleaner** started a series about once-thriving residential communities that have started to decay because of crime and other factors, such as the illegal operation of commercial activities.

The first community featured was Eastwood Park Gardens; it is illustrative of the fate of other residential communities in Kingston and throughout Jamaica: "Eighty-nine-year-old Clara Cole has lived most of her life on Westminster Road in Eastwood Park Gardens, Kingston, and is determined to see out the rest of her days in the community, even though the signs are clear that things are fast falling apart. Her former neighbour, Basil Wright, has seen enough of the decay of the once-solid middle- class community and has relocated to Mandeville, Manchester. "There is nothing that can be done at this stage," says Wright, who has put his Eastwood Park Gardens house on the market with a $16-million price tag. Cole, who uses a metal walker to move about the house she has occupied since age 15, agrees that the once-peaceful neighbourhood is going down. Cole noted that Eastwood Park Gardens has changed much since she was a teenager. "Before, the place was clean and quiet, and residents respected each other. Today, however, mostly because of an influx of commercial activity, the community has deteriorated into a ghost town," said Cole. "Something needs to be done. The Eastwood Park Citizens' Association has tried. They collected money to try to deal with it, but the commercial properties got worse," argued Cole, as she pointed out that the increase in commercial activities has driven initial homeowners from their properties. "They (business operators) go away in the evenings and there are few of us left here at night. We don't have anybody to call on if anything because the people gone home and the places are locked up," said Cole. "When I came here you had the nice homes, nicely kept with all the gardens and so on, and all the little children. You could find the nurses, those with babies, all meet up at the corner in the evenings and everyone was cordial," continued the woman. That scenery has changed, however, replaced by noisy machinery, expletives, and the constant smell of ganja smoke. Wright, who served as president of the Eastwood Park Gardens Citizens' Association for 17 years, is bitter that nobody did anything to stop the degradation of the area in the early stage. "When we bought this place in 1981, in the whole of Eastwood Park Gardens you could count five or six non-residential properties. Then everything started to change," said Wright. Like Cole, Barbara Thompson, who lives near the intersection of Lancaster Road and Sandringham Avenue, will have to suffer the commercialisation a bit longer. Having lived in the community for 35 years, she is angry that trailers that deliver goods to a nearby property have destroyed her once-thriving lawn as the drivers try to manoeuvre the huge vehicles into the commercial premises. Another resident, who asked that her name be withheld, likened today's Eastwood Park Gardens to the Riverton City dump. "Everything is here in Eastwood Park Gardens: you have obeah man, you have whorehouse, all kinds of businesses, and it is so bad," fumed the woman. "I know that businesses are here, but they can't be putting up the big old signs and disturbing people. When them leave they gone to Cherry Gardens and them place there. We don't have anywhere to go but here," charged the woman. Town clerk Robert Hill and members of the Kingston and St Andrew Corporation (KSAC) are well aware of the concerns of the residents, but Hill said not all the commercial properties are operating in breach of the law. "There are some commercial entities that exist there under permit from KSAC, but it is largely for mixed usage. In that respect, the community is still 80-odd percent residential," claimed Hill. "What has happened is that you have a series of illegal operators opening businesses where homes used to be, or converting residential structures into commercial structures," said Hill. "We have been monitoring them, and we have actually won a court case recently regarding a studio that was put there, and the court has ruled against the operators of the studio that they cease and vacate. "I know that the system is not moving as fast as we would like it but this is the court system that we have to work with. We are working on several (commercial properties) in that and other areas," added Hill. [Source: The Sunday Gleaner, 'A garden no more - Eastwood Park Gardens residents suffer in silence', March 18, 2015.

Improper Approvals

In keeping with Section 8 of the Building Act (2018) and Section 11 of the Town & Country Planning Act (1957), the Local Authorities (Municipal Corporations) are required to execute functions as Local Building and Planning Authorities in their respective jurisdictions. These functions include the:

1. Administration and enforcement of the Building Act, the National Building Code, and any other Regulations relevant to the Building Act;
2. Accept and consider applications for Building and Planning permission in respect of all proposed developments within its jurisdictions consistent with the Building Act and TCPA stipulations;
3. Grant permission for development either unconditionally, or subject to such conditions as they think fit, or refuse such applications. In dealing with such applications the Local Planning Authority shall have regard to the provisions of the Development Order so far as

material thereto, and to any other material considerations;

4. Accept and consider applications for building permission in respect of all proposed buildings within its area of jurisdiction to which this Act applies, and make determinations on the applications, subject to any term or condition that may be specified;

5. Ensure that all building work within its area of jurisdiction is carried out in accordance with the Building Act, the National Building Code, and any other regulations made under these statutes;

6. Issue certificates of compliance and certificates of occupancy in respect of buildings and building works;

7. Ensure that designs submitted in respect of Building and Planning applications are in compliance with the Building and TCP Acts, the National Building Code, and any other regulations made under these respective Acts, and that the design and supervisory aspects of building work are undertaken and executed by duly qualified persons; and

8. Perform such other functions as are necessary or expedient for, or in connection with, the proper performance of its functions under the requisite Acts, the National Building Code or any other regulations made under these Acts.

It is required that all the above-mentioned functions be undertaken conscientiously, ethically, professionally, and transparently.

The island's municipal corporations have received a total of 37,577 applications for processing since 2016 with the value of approved applications totalling more than $1.5 trillion. This information was disclosed on January 26, 2024, by the Mayor of Kingston, Senator Delroy Williams, during his contribution to the State of the Nation Debate in the Senate.

But things are far from rosy.

"For the second time in 2020, the Supreme Court of Jamaica has ruled in favour of corporate area communities where developers have trampled on the rights of citizens. We refer to judgments in the Birdsucker Drive development and, before that, the

Montrose project in the Golden Triangle, which handed wins to citizens and defeats for disorderly developments. These verdicts strike at the core of what appears to be rampant unregulated housing developments across Kingston and St. Andrew. The court agreed with the citizens that both the Kingston and St. Andrew Municipal Corporation (KSAMC) and environmental regulator National Environment and Planning Agency (NEPA) erred by granting approval" [Source: The Sunday Gleaner, December 20, 2020].

Lack of Monitoring & Enforcement

"Tis an unweeded garden that grows to seed; things rank and gross in nature." - William Shakespeare

The KSAMC – and all the other municipal corporations - has also been found wanting in its lack of monitoring of housing developments for which it has given approval.

The Gleaner noted in its editorial on January 15, 2024, that "In instances where permit violations have been uncovered, it has mostly been because of court actions, or persistent advocacy, citizen groups or individual neighbours, rather than oversight by regulators."

Citizens' Rights to the City (CRC), a group comprising representatives of citizens associations and individual residents of 29 communities in Kingston, has been stirred into action and has been making its voice heard concerning developments in their communities.

For example, in the Letter-of-the-Day in **The Gleaner** on December 7, 2022, the group bemoaned "An explosion in multistorey, residential development and commercial activity. The volume and pace are far ahead of the capacity of the KSAMC and other agencies to ensure compliance with building and planning laws. This is resulting in widespread breaches. Many negative impacts are being experienced. These include increased traffic and noise levels, less green space, loss of privacy, blocked natural air flow and light for neighbouring single-family dwellings, increased run-off from paved surfaces adding to more flooding, more garbage but limited collection, more pressure on inadequate water supplies, more sewage and water costs for older residents and others on limited fixed incomes, and high, speculative demand that is driving property costs out of the reach of most city dwellers." [Source: The Gleaner, 'Consider the rights of the citizens, Mr. PM', December 7, 2022]

11 Charlemont Drive

I am citing this case to illustrate the lax monitoring and enforcement of construction projects.

The case resulted from a probe by the Integrity Commission (IC) based on complaints by Charlemont Avenue, Kingston 6 neighbours.

From **The Gleaner** on January 14, 2024: "An investigation conducted by the Integrity Commission confirmed that NEPA issued building, planning, and environmental permits to Mark and Annette Barnett for the construction of two three-storey blocks consisting of 12 one-bedroom units at # 11 Charlemont Drive, St. Andrew. (Mark Barnett was at the time the President of the National Water Commission). However, Director of Investigations at the Integrity Commission Kevon Stephenson concluded, in a scathing 90-page report made public last October [2023, that the development, now listed as completed, consists of six two-bedroom units and six three-bedroom units, "in breach of the permits issued."

Whereas NEPA issued the environmental permits, the **KSAMC** issued the building permits.

I read the DPP's ruling in the 'Mark & Annette Barnett saga' in full. This stuck with me: "The disparity in the relevant observations of these two significant agencies (NEPA and the KSAMC) is quite concerning; NEPA, that is responsible for seeing to the environmental concerns of the country and KSAMC, who has the responsibility of managing and maintaining high standards in the building code, cannot be overlooked. The officer from NEPA observed and noted the breach on 17th December 2020 [after his 7th visit!], however, seven days prior, on 10th December 2020, Mr. David Clarke from the **KSAMC** visited the location and found that *"The building structure was compliant with the approved building plan issued by the KSAMC."*

The DPP ruled that although there was sufficient evidence that the permits were breached no criminal charges can be brought against them (the Barnetts) because the passage of time has made the case statute-barred. A case is statute-barred when the timeframe stipulated in law for it to be placed before the court has expired.

Instead, the DPP directed that the case against Barnett and his wife Annette be referred to the KSAMC to conduct an "administrative review" in accordance with the provisions of the Building Act, adding that "It is imperative that the actions of the office of the Chief Engineering Officer including the Senior Building Officer be assessed by the KSAMC and their parent ministry."

It was only after the ruling by the DPP that the limp KSAMC announced that "...the alleged construction breach by the President of the National Water Commission, Mark Barnett, and his wife, Annette, is currently the subject of an internal investigation. In a statement, the KSAMC says among the matters being investigated is the variation between the reports regarding the findings of the officers of the National Environment and Planning Agency (NEPA) and the municipal corporation regarding the construction of an apartment complex located at Charlemont Drive in St. Andrew. "Once these investigations are completed, the KSAMC will take all necessary and appropriate actions to ensure that the building and planning laws are enforced and adhered to. Further, it says it is involved in a dynamic and ongoing process of reviewing the administrative regime for building approvals, which has resulted in several measures taken to strengthen these processes." [Source: The Gleaner, January 12, 2024]

No Jamaican that I know thinks any meaningful change will result from the KSAMC's review.

Veteran Journalist Cliff Hughes disdainfully commented "Review my foot! Nothing will come of this review! Absolutely nothing. Besides, the KSAMC cannot review itself!"

Furthermore, civil society activist Carol Narcisse poured scorn on the KSAMC's announcement in a post on X (formerly Twitter) in these terms, "This is unconvincing and unacceptable. The reasons discrepant KSAMC reports are possible are documented in the IC report from October 2020. It lays bare the systemic malfunctions that need urgent fixing. This is so telling and such an indictment. The integrity Commission's report was provided in October 2023. From this release, the Council is telling us it didn't trouble itself with any internal process from then. The IC report sets out exactly the who, what and why. KSAMC itself needs investigating and not by themselves. The Council must be made to prioritise taking the steps to prosecute the Barnetts under the Building Act. Based on the IC's findings and substance of the ODPP report the lack of fidelity to duty, good practice, and the laws indicate that several public officers need firing."

In addition, in its editorial ('Beyond Charlemont, Mr. Mayor') of January 15, 2024, **The Gleaner** reminded the KSAMC and its chairman, Kingston Mayor Delroy Williams, that it had "Unfinished business, on related issues, to attend to." Said The Gleaner, "For example, Mr. Williams should report on the outcome of the case of two senior members of the corporation's building department who were, two years ago, in January 2022, interdicted and sent on leave by the Local Government Services Commission for unspecified concerns relating to construction oversight. One of those officials, Shawn Martin, a field inspector and second in command of planning, was heavily criticised in a 2020 ruling by Georgiana Fraser for his part in approving a development on Birdsucker Drive in Kingston 6, which the court said breached the regulations. The National Environment and Planning Agency (NEPA) was also lambasted in that ruling."

The KSAMC and NEPA must know now that their actions are under the microscope.

Public Parks

Public parks that fall under the purview of the municipal corporations are unkempt.

To wit: "Existing parks in the capital city, and across the entire country, have been shamefully neglected, and the expansion of quality green spaces has been cramped by Government, which doesn't think first class. High-quality public spaces may have something to do with the quality of people's lives and thoughts and actions." [Martin Henry, The Sunday Gleaner, December 2, 2018].

The Mandela Park in Half-Way-Tree is an embarrassment to the great man and his family. And his admirers. And to all well-thinking Jamaicans.

From **The Gleaner**: "Nelson Mandela would not give two hoots about the size of a park named in his honour, or if the space is really only "a little median" between two thoroughfares. What Mr. Mandela would care about is that the park, any park, or similar public facility, wherever located, is accessible to the public, regardless of race, class, or creed. And he would insist that the facility be well maintained and that its users be treated with decency and respect.

Mr. Mandela was rare among leaders. He eschewed bitterness. In power, he displayed grace and humility, without compromising conviction. He did not forget those who supported black South Africans in their battle for freedom. Significantly, in 1991 Jamaica was among the first countries he visited after being released. Half-Way Tree Park was renamed in his honour. The park is at the heart of one of the capital's critical transportation hubs and commercial centres. Like the areas around it, where once-pristine kiosks have grown ramshackle. It is often enveloped in the rank scent of urine. Mandela Park should be an oasis in the heart of a busy metropolis – a place where commuters should be able to pause and reflect. The area around the park and its immediate vicinity should be part of this embrace of the spirit of Nelson Mandela." [Source: The Gleaner, 'Mandela would not like it', May 26, 2022]

Street Vending

Because of the impotence of the Municipal Corporations, vending illegally has been normalised athwart Jamaica from Morant Bay in the eastern end of the country to Negril in the western end.

I agree with the sentiment expressed in this editorial from the **Jamaica Observer** newspaper: "Let us be abundantly clear that this newspaper is not for one second suggesting or even intimating that Jamaicans must not be given a chance to make an honest living. Absolutely not! We boldly and without equivocation encourage the entrepreneurial drive and spirit of all Jamaicans. But to do so at the expense of the rights and comfort of others is no longer acceptable. The various municipal corporations, as suggested by the mayors, have to aid the process by providing designated areas for vendors to ply their trade in a clean and environmentally friendly atmosphere. If this is not done in a timely manner, problems are going to occur, leading to possible conflicts, which are unwanted at this time. After these areas are designated, then the vendors must comply and use the space provided in the conduct of their businesses." [Source: Jamaica Observer Editorial, November 9, 2018]

The Town and Communities Act of 1884, although dated in several respects due to the effluxion of time, contains provisions to regulate street vending, but these are not enforced consistently by the Municipal

Corporations. The result is that street vending takes place just about anywhere in Jamaica regardless of the consequences.

Public Markets

A headline in **The Gleaner** read, *'Shoppers Shun Unsanitary MoBay Market, Say Vendors'*. Here are the gory details: "Dozens of disgruntled vendors who operate out of the Charles Gordon Market in Montego Bay are blaming the St. James Municipal Corporation and the market's management for shoppers refraining from using the facility because of deplorable and unsanitary conditions. The vendors claim that it has been months since the market was power-washed. "Not even pigs would survive in this sort of mud and unsanitary condition," said one vendor, who gave his name as Mikey Sawyers. "Mi deh a market wid mi mother from mi born, and this is the worst I have ever seen the market. Wi have to sell in a pure mud, and rain don't have to fall fi we in a mud. Not even a good pig farmer would raise his pigs in this yah condition." One female vendor, who identified herself only as Thelma, said that the holiday season was one of the worse they had experienced at the market. Unsanitary conditions at the Charles Gordon Market have been a recurring complaint from vendors over the years, with many calling for a more suitable location to accommodate them." [Source: The Gleaner, January 3, 2109]

The unsanitary conditions of the Charles Gordon Market in Montego Bay mirror similar conditions in the public markets right across Jamaica.

From Prof. Carolyn Cooper: "In my October 2019 [Gleaner] column, *"Papine Market stalls destroyed by KSAMC,"* I noted that, "The market's open-air concrete garbage dump is a complete disgrace. It seems as if garbage is not collected regularly. Every Friday and Saturday, the dump is piled high. If the KSAMC really wants to get rid of rubbish, the dump should be their priority, not the vendors' stalls. I proposed a viable solution to the problem: "Some enterprising person should set up a composting business in markets across Jamaica. So much foodstuff goes to waste! It could all be recycled and turned into valuable fertiliser instead of adding to the high volume of solid waste that ends up in dumps. And valuable jobs could be easily created from recycling. It just takes imagination."

In January 2024, under the caption *'Papine Market dump a stinking disgrace'*, Professor Cooper wrote, "Two Saturdays ago, I visited the Papine Market. The dump was even worse than I remembered it (in 2019). The mountain of garbage had overflowed on to the sidewalk. And the smell! It really can't be healthy to buy food near that dump. I took photos of the Papine Market dump which I emailed last Friday to His Worship the Mayor, Councillor Delroy Williams, and copied to several members of his staff. When I followed up with a call, I was told he was at a sitting of the Senate. I viewed on YouTube the recording of the mayor's wide-ranging presentation, which included remarks on the issue of garbage collection." [Source: The Gleaner, January 27, 2024]

The poor management of public markets by the Municipal Corporations is another example that makes clear they are bereft of the capacity for shame and that they scan as being grossly incompetent.

Fire Hydrants

Well-maintained and functioning fire hydrants are the exception if they can be found any at all, from Morant Bay in the eastern end of the island to Negril Point in the western end.

Reader, if you think I am exaggerating, consider this: in an article published in **The Sunday Gleaner** on December 17, 2017, it was stated that "More than

3,600 of the 13,529 hydrants across the island were not working."

Just pause and think about the implications of this for public safety.

Public Cemeteries

"Their condition shows contempt for the dead and the grieving."

Right across the island, the lack of maintenance of public cemeteries has left them in a state of utter and complete disgrace! I am not exaggerating. Driving past them is a source of recurring cringe to me, and I'm sure it is the same for other persons.

'Stunned by 'Forest', Trelawny Expat Adopts Martha Brae Cemetery' was the banner headline of a story carried by **The Gleaner** on December 5, 2019: "Shocked at the run-down state of the four main cemeteries in Trelawny, a Jamaican expatriate has committed to clean the burial ground in her hometown of Martha Brae because of the failure of municipal authorities. Judy Doctor, who lives in the United States, said she was so stunned by the unkempt condition when she visited the tomb of her father, former Trelawny cricketer Vincent Doctor, in June that she paid out of pocket to have the cemetery cleaned up.

"I could hardly find a place to walk. It was a forest of trees and shrubs," said Doctor. "I arranged and paid to have the whole cemetery cleaned, so when Wendell Stewart died, he was buried in a freshly clean cemetery," she told **The Gleaner**, referring to the former member of parliament for North Trelawny who died on November 10. "I was at his interment and heard several persons expressing delight at how clean the cemetery was. One woman said it was the first time in several years that she had seen the cemetery this clean," the now Virginia resident said.

The 'forest' that the Martha Brae Cemetery had become, and which stirred Judy Doctor to act, accurately describes **all** public cemeteries across Jamaica, including the one in my hometown of Ewarton, St. Catherine.

When I was growing up, the Ewarton Cemetery was organised and well-maintained, but now it is a congested, disordered, and messy place – utter chaos set in permanence.

On January 23, 2023, I attended a funeral at the Ewarton Cemetery. To say that I was shocked at the terrible state it was in would be a colossal understatement. I took photographs. The following day, I shared the photographs on my Facebook page and my thoughts in a post titled **'They Lack the Capacity for Shame'**:

"I'm sure that, without an explanation, you will be hard-pressed to figure out what these photographs are depicting. I will forgive you for thinking that you are looking at the early growth stages of a forest because that is exactly what the Ewarton Cemetery is! It is in a deplorable and disgraceful condition! Chacka, chacka, and wholly disordered. Look at the photos again. I grew up in Ewarton. When I was a likkle boy, the Cemetery was an organized place. There was a road in the 'middle' of it where hearses could drive into it to unload coffins. There was also a covered, paved area (a 'chapel' where services for the 'unchurched' could be held or where people could shelter if it rained). The Cemetery also had 'zones' reserved for the different Churches. The road and the 'chapel' are gone - graves now occupy these areas, and the rest of the cemetery, in a haphazard manner like bricks dumped from the back of a truck. It is an anxiety-inducing and breath-stopping sight to behold pallbearers manouvering over old graves to get to newly made ones without spilling corpses from coffins. Locals tell me that new graves being placed on top of old ones (of unrelated people) is now routinely being done. Graves have also been built practically on the main road. And then there are the weeds and overgrown trees that are the dominant feature of the cemetery now! It is an unmitigated disgrace! Chaos set in permanence. It boggles the mind and creates a profound dissonance that an entity with responsibility for the cemetery exists! This entity is the St. Catherine Municipal Corporation. And its leadership, starting with the mayor (his so-called 'worship') is utterly and completely devoid of the capacity for shame! For allowing the Ewarton Cemetery to be reduced to such a disgraceful state."

More on the disgraceful state of public cemeteries: "One of my occupations takes me often to burial grounds. Apart from the very expensive private cemeteries, public burial facilities are generally in a disgraceful condition. What is the justification for expensive Municipal Corporations and a ministry of local government if they can't even manage the decent disposal of human remains? They show contempt for the dead and the grieving by poor management of these basic public health facilities-invariably overcrowded, overgrown, and unsupervised? No wonder Mr. Seaga wanted the whole lot abolished two generations ago." ~ Rev. Ronnie Thwaites, The Gleaner March 27, 2023

The neglect of public cemeteries by the Municipal Corporations is another example that makes it clear that they are bereft of the capacity for shame and scan as incompetent acolytes of mediocrity and co-conspirators of chaos.

Unplanned Developments

On Thursday, January 31, 2019, 2-year-old twin girls Nahelia and Nahalia Pinnock were burnt to death when a fire broke out in their house in the inner-city community of Grant's Pen in Kingston. The fire service (The Jamaica Fire Brigade) was quick on the scene, but because of the unplanned nature of the community firemen were unable to get close to the house to effectively put out the blaze. When the fire was eventually extinguished, it was reported that the "Bodies of the babies were seen with smoke coming from them."

Reader, I cried when I read the report.

One public commentator who is familiar with the Grants Pen community visited a few days after the fire and described it as a case study in concentrated long-term (i.e., intergenerational) poverty.

Here is his heart-breaking account: "Two Fridays ago, I visited and saw residents there using shovels to clean up the charred remains of the hovels they lived in and the possessions they owned. What immediately struck me, even though I have walked on the outskirts of the community before, was how close the housing units were to each other. People were literally living on top of each other. It seems unimportant to the person who has the physical space to spare, but as I walked through a section of the burnt-out ruins, I could feel and see in my mind the people constantly living and breathing in the fetid claustrophobic air that made them feel as if they were lesser beings. People jam-packed against each other has never been a recipe for good social outcomes. We who live uptown or even in rural hills where our personal space is guaranteed could never spend more than one night in Grants Pen. I could not. And if it is not good enough for me, why should it be considered satisfactory for the residents – man, woman, child, and toddler."

Also, when prime minister Andrew Holness visited a section of the community of Tivoli Gardens, a Jamaica Labour Party (JLP) stronghold, ironically, in December 2019, he was compelled to confess to the residents that, "Your conditions here are not something that the Government is proud of."

What are the 'conditions' to which the prime minister felt ashamed? Veritable hovels! That's what thousands of Jamaicans are consigned to live in ... hovels ... decrepit communities ... poor infrastructure ... persistent misery, and the unrelenting shame of dehumanising poverty.

Isn't this social genocide?

An estimated 900,000 people, or nearly a third of the population, live in squatter or informal settlements, characterised by inadequate access to basic amenities. Living hurts in these communities.

In an essay titled *"A Case for Adequate Housing: Achieving Sustainable Development Goal 11 in Caribbean Small Island Development States,"* Prof. Carol Archer and Dr. Anetheo Grant-Jackson of the Faculty of the Built Environment, University of Technology, Jamaica, outlined the attributes established by the United Nations for adequate housing, namely: "Security of tenure, which is essential to ensure freedom from forced eviction, risk of demolition; availability and access to housing services, facilities and infrastructure; affordability; habitability; equal and non-discriminatory access for all; location, in terms of access to employment, healthcare, schools and other social services; and cultural adequacy." [Source: State of the Tropics Report 2020, Thomas Cook University]

In the same essay I mentioned above, Prof. Archer and Dr. Grant-Jackson noted that "Jamaica has a record of persistent housing shortages, a proliferation of squatter settlements and poor housing conditions (and) this reflects the failure of both the private and public sectors' housing outputs to meet the standard of adequate housing for all. The most pervasive housing challenges on the supply side include, among others, land availability and access, institutional arrangements, and legal frameworks for housing, building construction and material costs, building standards, housing finance and incentives for developers. On the demand side, challenges relate to income levels and housing affordability; population size and composition; and householders' preferences."

A key takeaway for me from the essay by Prof. Archer and Dr. Grant-Jackson is that "One of the most observable symptoms of inadequate housing is the proliferation of informal dwellings and settlements"!

There is a particular informal community that I've watched mushroom right under the figurative noses of the local authorities. It has no planned infrastructure – roads, water supplies, sewage, and so forth.

Reader, consider this: On March 18, 2020, a television crew from a local media house visited a 'tenement yard' ('big yard') in one of Kingston's gritty inner-city communities. It was revealed that 40 persons lived in the dilapidated collection of rickety shacks. A 44-year-old woman, who was mother to eight children and 10 grandchildren, shared the following disturbing reality with the TV crew: "Mi nuh have nuh bathroom enuh, a pipe-side mi bathe. And mi nuh have nuh toilet either, a bucket mi use and dump it inna manhole."

Concerned citizen, Winston Barrett, CEO of Corporate Interiors International Ltd., troubled by what he sees around him as he goes out and about, felt compelled to pen this: "Let us give people back their dignity. The next budget must make provisions to address these glaring examples of neglect. I hate when I drive on certain roads and see people disappearing behind zinc fences into little hovels that are their homes. This make me so sad, I often remark to myself that, imagine, after over 50 years of Independence, this is all we can do for our people. We need real, comprehensive, anti-poverty programmes, more than what the Jamaica Social Investment Fund (JSIF) and PATH Programme do, although these are useful. I am recommending programmes on the scale of what Lula da Silva did in Brazil and Deng Xiaping did in China after Mao died." [Source: The Gleaner, March 16, 2020].

Meanwhile, the political 'misleaders' live in opulence and luxury. Prime Minister Holness has built a mansion. Jamaican politicians enjoy the best quality of life possible in Jamaica. The cruel irony is that they are supported by the blood, sweat, and tears of the Jamaican people. After 60 years of Independence!

What is also noteworthy is that the aforementioned Grants Pen community is another stark example of the 'two Jamaicas' that coexist uneasily – it is surrounded by some of Jamaica's most affluent gated communities. The Member of Parliament is the Minister of Justice, a Rhodes Scholar, and an Attorney-at-Law.

The stark bifurcation of Jamaican society has long been recognised: "In 1961, in the Jamaican House of

Assembly, a relatively young Edward Seaga, then opposition member, raised the uncomfortable issue of class division in the Jamaican society in his famous 'Haves vs Have-Nots' speech. Seaga was troubled by the depressed state of living of the majority of Jamaicans while a small majority had opulent lifestyles. Seaga observed that the expenditure of one middle-class family was able to cover the expenses of many families in what he termed the "have-nots" portion of society. Fast-forward to 2019. A young opposition senator, Damion Crawford, ignited similar sentiments when he observed at a mass rally for the People's National Party (PNP) on March 3, 2019, that 'the system' is stacked against too many ordinary Jamaicans who are living in very depressed conditions while a small minority enjoys the benefits of economic growth. Crawford's observation is grounded in data that show that the average consumption spend by persons in the lowest, income quintiles is J$153,000 per year while the average for persons in the highest-income quintiles is J$456,000 per year. This is akin to Seaga's observation over 50 years ago that the 'haves' spending could easily feed multiple families in Jamaica at the time. In today's Jamaica, the data show that what one family in the 'haves' group spends on consumption can feed three families per year in the 'have-not' group." [Prof. Densil Williams, The Gleaner, March 17, 2019]

Here's more on Jamaica's stark and savage inequality: "Do you have a drone? If you do, launch it and slow it down on a section of Riverton City where you may see a picture in frame after frame of five children sorting glass bottles, metals of various shapes, or old electronic units as others with digging tools pass it to them. You will notice that the children, although working for 10 hours daily, do not openly express dissatisfaction as they sort stuff one piece after the other. A lot more is at play that cannot be captured by a mere drone. In other words, some may be sad and in social pain but not all are unhappy. An hour later, move your drone to a fancy hill community. A party is on. Pre-coronavirus or in the present there is a poolside gathering. Pity the drone cannot capture the smell of barbecued wild hog and grilled lobster. Many of those at that gathering are happy and socially and economically filled, but not all are happy. We have long been fed the diet that there are two Jamaicas. It's more like about four

Jamaica ... [Source: Mark Wignall, 'Suffering and the two Jamaicas,' The Gleaner, March 26, 2021]

Jamaica's official motto is 'Out of Many, One People'. However, in reality it is 'Out of Many, One Stratified People'.

By sheer serendipity, I was driven through one of Jamaica's uber-exclusive gated communities. At the entrance, a uniformed security guard performed duties filtering entrants and, in the process, ensuring that no 'undesirable non-belongers' got inside. Fate had orchestrated that I bear witness to 'social filtering' in action! I was a visitor to another 'oasis Jamaica,' the other one being the 'All-inclusive' hotels. Perhaps because I was visiting 'this Jamaica' for the first time, having spent 99.99% of my life in 'another Jamaica,' the 'dividing line' became visible to me.

To be sure, other evidence of 'social separation' in Jamaica exists! But, it was as if before, in a kind of dysconscious state, a peculiar kind of stupor, I had acclimated to it. But I was now 'woke' to it driving through this uber-exclusive enclave, which was a reification of social division. Perched on top of a long, dry limestone mountain, residents of this enclave have a panoramic view of the city of Kingston, with the towering and well-vegetated mountain as its backdrop.

The bespoke houses were attractive, as they reposed in the warm, tropical colours in which they were painted. Enveloped by a richness of pretty flowers seen only in tropical paradises, they all sat on landscaped and regularly manicured lawns. As complementary symbols of claimed and announced elevated status and class, late model, high-end motor vehicles adorned the front of all the houses, telegraphing the 'social arrival' of their owners. The experience confirmed in real terms that it is true that more than one Jamaica truly exists. In further processing my experience from my visit to this Jamaica, it occurred to me that 'social class' is reflected in the lived reality of how different segments of a population experience their country.

The exclusive enclave was a safe space that starkly contrasted with the many violent and shambolic communities, such as the iconic Trench Town, where the daily lived reality of many other Jamaicans is different.

Writing in the **Jamaica Observer** newspaper on January 5, 2020, Keith Duncan, CEO of Jamaica Money Market Brokers Group and President of the

Private Sector Organization of Jamaica (PSOJ), in an article titled *'Jamaica's reality and achieving Vision 2030,'* wrote the following: "My children have grown up insulated from the harsh realities of Jamaica and some of us in our more privileged domains really look at the crime and murder rates and poverty levels as statistics until it comes too close to home. Over the Christmas holidays, I decided that I wanted to expose my children to some of the realities of Jamaica. As they can easily identify with Bob Marley, I took them to visit the Trench Town Culture Yard Museum. While I knew that poverty was a real problem in Jamaica, what my sons and I observed was abject poverty. The hopelessness that existed was depressing, to say the least."

The foregoing is remarkable. To begin with, it is yet further confirmation that 'two Jamaicas' – a dual society - exist. And I think it is also a patronizing admission of how 'well-heeled' Jamaicans treat poor Jamaicans as objects of fascination, akin to taking their children to view 'interesting' creatures in a Zoo. This is faux virtue-signalling.

For some people, Jamaica is truly paradise – heaven on earth! For others, Jamaica is a veritable paradox – a place that imposes a heavy allostatic load, psychic injury, and social suffering on them to daily schlep.

So, Edward Seaga spoke about the 'haves and the have nots' in 1961. Yet, the situation has not changed *fundamentally* in contemporary Jamaica – the historical chassis remains. It is certainly one country but of parallel universes of starkly contrasting realities.

"Dens of Corruption"

In its 2022-2023 Annual Report, The Integrity Commission reported that the compliance rate for the filing of Statutory Declarations by Councillors was 72%.

The annual Integrity Commission examination of the income, assets and liabilities of Councillors, members of parliament, and other public officials is one basic tool democracies use globally in tracking whether public officials are getting rich illicitly at public expense.

Former Contractor General, Dirk Harrison, described the Municipal Corporations, writ large, as "Dens of corruption."

In a 2007 study by the Caribbean Policy Research Institute (CAPRI), the top five most perceived corrupt groups were the police, **parish councils**, customs, central government, and public works.

In a case concerning the fraudulent conversion of more than $400 million of public funds, the deputy superintendent of road and works of the Manchester Municipal Corporation, his wife, and his parents are the defendants. An entire family. A family affair. Other defendants include the secretary-manager and director of finance, and the works overseer. The diabolical and creative shenanigans they allegedly used to siphon off massive amounts of taxpayers' funds – hundreds of millions - for their own benefits and asset-stacking are mind-boggling. Prosecutors submitted that the former deputy superintendent of roads and works at the corporation, made credit card purchases of luxury brands, including Prada, Louis Vuitton, Lacoste, Guess, Foot Locker, Armani, Perry Ellis, and Timberland while on vacation overseas. Hotel stays, purchase of luxury cars, millions in investments on the stock market, and property construction were also revealed among the expenditures. The lead prosecutor said that his $255 million net worth is not substantiated by his wages from the corporation but was built through monies swindled from the corporation. It was reiterated that from 2008 up to his arrest in 2016, he would have earned just under $15 million; bank deposits showed signs of significant earnings increase from 2012, around the time he would have been promoted to deputy superintendent, and, at one point, acting superintendent at the corporation [Source: The Gleaner, January 17, 2020].

And in a twist that has raised eyebrows, a fire that reportedly started in the Judge's Chambers caused $35 million worth of damage to the Manchester Parish Court during the trial.

Thankfully, at the end of the trial, three former officials at the Manchester Municipal Corporation and two of their co-accused were convicted for their roles in a fraud scheme that fleeced the local government authority approximately $400 million.

It is believed to be the biggest fraud case at a municipal authority in Jamaica's history. The trial lasted more than eight months and 46 witnesses were called, and 249 documents were admitted. The scheme involved the use of fictitious invoices for the payment of monies for services that were never provided. [Source: The Gleaner, May 15, 2020]

Transforming the Municipal Corporations

****

Poor governance is at the root of Jamaica's intractable problems. The incompetence of the Municipal Corporations evinces this. Therefore, they must be transformed and reimagined.

Below, I curate some prescriptions for transforming them.

Abolish the Fiction

In Jamaica, 'local government' is a fiction. There is an incongruously named cabinet 'Ministry of Local Government & Community Development' at the national level that controls the Municipal Corporations and funds them through a Parochial Revenue Fund (PRF). The PRF is a source of funds the Ministry of Local Government doles out into the coffers of the municipal corporations as if it were a parent giving a child an allowance. But these are funds that originate from property tax and tax on motor vehicles that originate at the local level in the different parishes.

On January 14, 2020, a Councillor in the Westmoreland Municipal Corporation, Ian Myles, wailed publicly that the corporation, not having received funds for more than three months, was being starved of funding from the Ministry of Local Government. The Councillor even intimated that there was the possibility of political victimisation because the corporation had a majority of members from the Opposition Political Party [Source: The Gleaner, 'Little London Councillor wants equity in parochial fund distribution'].

For years there has been talk of 'Local Government Reform," but the process has been endlessly drawn out, and has now petered out, and is not even discussed anymore. Over the years, many reform proposals have been put forward, but they have all suffered stillbirth.

In 1993 an effort to reform local Government resulted in Ministry Paper No. 8/93 which stated: "The need for fundamental [Local Government] reform has been on the national agenda for the last 50 years, during which seven major studies [were] conducted. These Studies have been remarkably unanimous in finding that the major contributors to [Local Government's] deficiencies and poor performance have been inadequate financing and lack of autonomy. Their recommendations have been consistent in emphasizing the need to provide

Local Authorities with adequate and independent sources of revenue and to grant them greater autonomy in the management of local affairs. Few of these recommendations have been accepted and/or implemented. Rather, the situation of Local Government has deteriorated over the years, both in respect to financing and autonomy."

The Ministry Paper set out the following "specific objectives of the Reform Programme:

1. Restoration of functions and responsibilities which were removed from Local Government, and rehabilitation of the Councils.
2. Establishment of new arrangements for the financing of Local Government which will allocate to them adequate and independent sources of revenue, and will give Local Authorities effective control over these sources of revenue.
3. To upgrade the institutional capability of Local Authorities to ensure that they are able to perform their functions in an efficient and cost-effective manner, and are enabled to take on the new challenge of providing leadership and coordination in the process of community development and empowerment.

4. To effect a comprehensive revision of all outdated legislation which presently constitute a major constraint to the effective performance of the Councils.

5. To upgrade the quality and cost-efficiency of all Local Government services and regulatory functions.

6. To shift the focus of Local Authorities to one of providing leadership and a coordinating framework to the collective efforts of the people of their respective Parishes, towards local development.

7. To examine the present distribution of service responsibilities between Central and Local Government, community organizations, NGOs, and the private sector, and to identify better or more cost-effective arrangements for the delivery of these services."

Additionally, Professor Rex Nettleford, former Vice-Chancellor of The University of the West Indies, led the National Advisory Council on local governance and produced a report in 2007 that was referred to as the "local government reform road-map." The report contained recommendations recommendations to address the following areas:

Democracy, Participation and Accountability; Finance and Funding of Local Government; Accounting and Financial Management; and the Structure and Functions of Local Government. The report also made strong recommendations for the entrenchment of Local Government in the Jamaican Constitution; the formulation of a National Policy on Decentralization; as well as the retention of the Parish Development Committees (PDC) model as the primary vehicle for facilitating participatory local governance. [Source: Jamaica Information Service]. Alas, the recommendations were not implemented.

I know of at least one individual who has benefitted bigly from this 'elasticised' process – he was a consultant engaged for an umpteenth number of years to drive the 'reform' process.

In 2016, a new Local Governance Act was passed. It is a significant piece of legislation aimed at decentralizing governance by empowering local authorities to manage their own affairs more effectively. It establishes Parish Municipal Corporations as the primary entities responsible for local governance. These Corporations are granted various powers and functions, including the management of local services, infrastructure, and development projects within their respective jurisdictions.

The Act outlines mechanisms for the election and composition of Parish Councils, as well as provisions for their financial management and accountability. Additionally, it emphasizes community participation in decision-making processes and aims to enhance transparency and efficiency in local governance across Jamaica.

One objective of this Act was to "Enhance [Local Authorities'] capacity to more effectively manage local affairs, with an expanded and more holistic mandate for the good governance, sustainable development and maintenance of good civic order within their respective jurisdictions and for connected matters, by enabling them to exercise powers and perform functions assigned to them."

The Act aims to achieve several objectives:

1. **Strengthening of the Local Government Institutions:** The act seeks to strengthen local government bodies in Jamaica, empowering them to effectively carry out their functions and responsibilities.

2. **Enhancing Local Decision-Making:** It aims to enhance local decision-making processes by granting greater autonomy and authority to local government entities. This includes giving them more control over local resources and decision-making related to local development priorities.
3. **Improving Service Delivery:** The Act intends to improve service delivery at the local level by promoting efficiency, accountability, and transparency in the management and delivery of public services.
4. **Promoting Local Development**: It seeks to promote local development initiatives by empowering local government authorities to plan, implement, and monitor development projects tailored to the specific needs of their communities.
5. **Encouraging Citizen Participation**: The Act encourages increased citizen participation in local governance processes, including decision-making, planning, and monitoring of local government activities.
6. **Ensuring Equity and Inclusivity:** It aims to ensure equity and inclusivity in the distribution of resources and benefits, thereby addressing

disparities between urban and rural areas and promoting social justice at the local level.

7. **Building Capacity:** The Act includes provisions for building the capacity of local government officials and staff to effectively perform their roles and responsibilities.

Overall, the Jamaica Local Governance Act of 2016 seeks to modernize and strengthen the local governance framework in Jamaica, with the ultimate goal of promoting sustainable development, improving quality of life, and enhancing democratic governance at the local level.

However, as noted by Attorney-at-Law Gordon Robinson in **The Gleaner** on February 14, 2024, under the new Act "The Minister received wide-ranging powers over municipal corporations including to institute proceedings to remove a Mayor after misconduct allegations made to the Minister. 'Responsibilities' were to be undertaken after 'consultation' and 'collaboration' with, inter alia, MPs!"

To the point made by Gordon Robinson, the Local Governance Act of 2016 outlines various powers and responsibilities for the Minister responsible for local government. Some of the powers vested in the Minister under this act may include:

1. **Policy Development**: The Minister is typically responsible for developing policies related to local governance, including regulations, guidelines, and frameworks for effective local administration.

2. **Appointment of Local Authorities**: The Minister may have the authority to appoint members of local authorities, such as municipal corporations or parish councils, or to approve their appointments.

3. **Budget Approval:** The Minister may have a role in approving the budgets of local authorities, ensuring that they are consistent with national priorities and guidelines.

4. **Oversight and Supervision:** The Minister often exercises oversight and supervision over the operations of local authorities to ensure compliance with relevant laws, regulations, and policies.

5. **Intervention Powers:** In cases where a local authority is unable to fulfill its responsibilities effectively or is facing challenges, the Minister may have the power to intervene, such as by

appointing a board of management or taking other corrective actions.

6. **Resource Allocation:** The Minister may play a role in allocating resources to local authorities, including financial resources, infrastructure development funds, or other forms of support.

7. **Policy Guidance:** Providing guidance to local authorities on matters such as planning, development control, service delivery, and community engagement.

8. **Coordination with Central Government:** Facilitating coordination and collaboration between local authorities and central government agencies to ensure effective service delivery and development planning at the local level.

The perception among a large swath of the electorate is that a concentration of authority in the central government makes the parish-based municipal authorities largely ineffectual.

Reimagining Local Government

Dr. Louis Moyston, writing in **The Gleaner** on February 7, 2024, on the heels of the announcement that the Local Government Election would be held on February 26, 2024, stated "What I cannot hear from both political parties is their perspectives on local government that has been through so many changes. The time has come for new discussions on conceptualising a new approach to local government and its critical role in rural development. The centralisation of local government in Jamaica has unleashed severe adverse consequences in rural Jamaica. In many countries, people have access to their local government leaders, as opposed to those from central government. There is a saying that "all politics is local". We need to redevelop the concept of local government with new areas of responsibilities, including playing a pivotal role in rural development, as well as ensuring equity in the spending of taxes and other resources in the rural parts, as opposed to the disproportionate spending of all taxes collected in the Corporate Area and tourists towns"

Dr. Moyston continued "A robust local government is also important in the process of democratisation, and by having increased people's participation in policy decision-making process. It must also play an important role in ensuring the effective allocation of tax resources in the rural parts, as well as the inspiring of the well-needed trust between the people and their political leaders. It is time for local government to take on new responsibilities in public services, health, education, and public education and the economy. There is also the need to upgrade the quality of leadership at the local government level in order to prepare that form of government for its new role, and that is, its participation in rural economic, social and political development in the quest to rebuild and strengthening rural communities that will contribute to the construction of a Jamaica developed, strong and free. It is most important for the PNP councillors to unite with the JLP local representatives on this issue. We have to inspire real development and transformation of Jamaica and its people, with the local government playing a most effective role in rural administration and development."

I agree wholeheartedly with Dr, Moyston and I am adding another dimension to the reimagined, which is the need for a 'new type' of Councillor, as described below.

Needed: A 'New Type' of Councillor

Councillors with a new profile and mindset are needed to be local government representatives. For starters, they need to be educated, open-minded, tech-savvy, and so forth.

In July 2023, Jamaica witnessed this jaw-dropping spectacle: A Councillor belonging to the St. Catherine Municipal Corporation was recorded delivering a keynote address at a primary school graduation in Old Harbour. The Councillor appeared to be struggling mightily to simply read the speech from his script.

And in January 2024, the Mayor of Port Antonio, in an interview on Nationwide Radio, was unable to demonstrate competence in simple arithmetic concerning allocations of funds made by the Portland Municipal Corporations.

More. A Councillor-candidate that I know puts his illiteracy on display daily in a neighbourhood WhatsApp group.

There is a crisis of confidence in the Municipal Corporations among the citizens. Yes, Jamaica needs a new crop of Councillors with a mind space completely different from those we have had and still have!

Under a new compensation system announced by the Ministry of Finance in 2023, the salaries of Councillors were increased from $1.7 million per annum to $5 million as of April 1, 2023. They will earn $5.7 million as of April 2024. In addition, a mayor's pay has increased from $3.3 million to $7.7 million. It will climb to approximately $10 million in 2024. The salaries for the mayors of Kingston and Montego are slightly higher than those of other mayors. [Source: The Gleaner, July 13, 2023]

Based on their comprehensive incompetence, how on earth do Municipal Corporations justify their call on resources? And their salaries?

Local government, as presently structured, is expensive foolishness.

Given the significant pay increase they have received, will we likely see a new and improved crop of Councillors in the Municipal Corporations anytime soon? I mean, Councillors who can at least put two sentences together coherently? Councillors who can orchestrate the efficient delivery of basic services to citizens?

Besides, I verily think young aspirants to political office, instead of seeking election directly to the House of Representatives as a member of parliament, should first run for the office of Councillor, learn the ropes, and establish a track record. Thereafter, if they wish to run for higher office, they would have had some experience and a record of performance on which they may be evaluated.

The truth is that I am seeing a ray of hope in some of the candidates contesting the 2024 Local Government Elections. Several of them have undergraduate and graduate degrees and are relatively young. The biggest problem though is that they will have to overcome a calcified system thrumming with mediocrity.

Needed: Clarification of Roles

As noted by Kristen Gyles in **The Gleaner** on December 21, 2023, "Every now and again there are bitter disagreements between Councillors and their MPs, whether over inadequate consultations before the commencement of infrastructural projects or just misaligned perspectives on what taxpayers' funds should be used for. We all know Councillors and MPs should be working together, but the fact is, in many cases, they don't. Instead, it seems the emerging norm is for Councillors to threaten to resign because of friction between themselves and MPs or MP caretakers."

On 'X' (formerly Twitter), I saw where an MP listed her achievements in the constituency she represents; all the listed things are things that fall within the remit of the local authorities.

Over the years, as noted by Attorney-at-Law Gordon Robinson in **The Gleaner** on February 14, 2024, "Councillors have become de facto representatives of MPs instead of divisions while MPs have become representatives of political parties instead of constituents."

Clearly, the lines of demarcation between the remit of the Councillor and that of the Member of Parliament need to be respected.

Outdated Laws

One of the fundamental recommendations of the Rex Nettleford-chaired National Advisory Committee on Local Government Reform was the need for a comprehensive revision of the legislations relating to Local Government. There are some eighty (80) Laws relating to local government, many of which are dated in the 19th Century.

Towns and Communities Act

This Act was passed in 1843. I have singled it out for mention because, although it is 'dated' in several respects (for example, it mentions horse-drawn carriages), it contains many provisions that remain useful in regulating conduct in public spaces, which if enforced by the Municipal Corporations, would eliminate the chaos that has been normalised athwart Jamaica's towns and communities.

Here are a few of the provisions:

Every person who:

- "Shall in any thoroughfare in any town, ride or drive furiously, or on any thoroughfare or highway ride or drive so as to endanger the life or limb of any person, or to the common danger of the passengers therein";
- "Shall, without consent of the owner or occupier affix any bill or paper against or upon any building, wall, fence or pale, or write upon, soil, deface, or mark any building, wall, fence, or pale in any other way whatsoever";
- "Shall, in any thoroughfare or public place, indecently expose his or her person";

- "Shall sell or distribute, or offer for sale or distribution, or shall mark on any fence, wall or any building, any obscene figure, drawing, painting, or representation, or sing any profane, indecent or obscene song or ballad, or write or draw any indecent or obscene word, figure, or representation, or use any profane, indecent or obscene language";
- "Shall loiter in any public place and solicit any person for the purpose of prostitution";
- "Shall burn any wood, shavings, rubbish, or sweepings in any street, lane or road" ... ***Shall be guilty of an offence and shall be liable to a penalty not exceeding one thousand dollars***.

Other provisions relate to "Exposing goods for sale in thoroughfares, etc."; "Exposing goods for sale on piazzas without the owners' consent"; "Riotous behaviour in public places while drunk"; "Noisy or disorderly conduct in public places"; "Mad dogs"; and "Street musicians."

None of the abovementioned provisions of the TCA are being enforced currently by the Municipal Corporations. Therefore, priority should be given to updating this useful piece of legislation, including the fines! And then enforcing the provisions.

****

My Closing Argument

When we fail to see the connection between things, we fail to anticipate the consequences of any one thing.

The contemporary reality in Jamaica concerning good governance and effective public administration by Jamaica's Local Government Authorities, the Municipal Corporations, is a pathetic one. This is because the Municipal Corporations are individually and collectively ineffective.

Their pervasive incompetence from Morant Bay in eastern Jamaica to Negril in the west is inescapable.

Today, disorder is evident everywhere and is commonly associated with, and is a blot on, the Jamaican brand. This disorder is largely the result of the gross ineptitude of the Municipal Corporations.

Because of the collective impotence of the Municipal Corporations, Jamaicans have shunned them at election time; this is reflected in low voter turnout.

However, given that Jamaica is a democratic society, the people, the citizens, must perform the duties and responsibilities that include, among other things, being hypervigilant concerning the country's affairs. Citizens must not abdicate or refrain from undertaking these duties and responsibilities.

Therefore, concerning elected officials who serve at the local government level in the Municipal Corporations, citizens must, by their actions, make it pellucidly clear that they are the real bosses of Jamaica, and we must hold them accountable. Staying away from local government elections will not catalyse change. Active participation in local governance will.

The Jamaica Local Government Act, 2016, outlines various roles and responsibilities for citizens within the local governance structure.

Some of the main roles of citizens under the Act include:

1. **Participation in Local Government Elections**: Citizens have the right to participate in local government elections by voting for their preferred candidates to represent them at the local level. These representatives include Councillors and Mayors.

2. **Engagement in Local Decision-Making**: Citizens have the opportunity to engage in

local decision-making processes through various mechanisms such as community meetings, town hall forums, and consultations organized by local authorities. They can provide input, feedback, and suggestions on matters affecting their communities.

3. **Demanding Accountability:** Citizens have the right to hold local government officials accountable for their actions and decisions. This includes monitoring the performance of elected representatives, reporting any instances of corruption or misconduct, and demanding transparency in the management of local resources.

4. **Participation in Community Development**: Citizens can actively participate in community development initiatives facilitated by local authorities. This may involve volunteering for local projects, contributing resources, or providing expertise to address local needs and challenges.

5. **Accessing Local Services:** Citizens have the right to access basic services provided by local government authorities, such as waste

management, sanitation, road maintenance, public transportation, and recreational facilities. They can also raise concerns or complaints regarding the quality or availability of these services.

6. **Compliance with Local Regulations:** Citizens are expected to comply with local regulations, by-laws, and ordinances established by the local government. This includes adhering to zoning laws, building codes, environmental regulations, and other policies aimed at maintaining order and promoting the well-being of the community.

Overall, the Jamaica Local Government Act emphasizes the importance of citizen participation, accountability, and collaboration in the governance of local communities, aiming to foster democracy, transparency, and effective service delivery at the grassroots level.

Indeed, if we look at history we will see that change occurs when changemakers decide that the moment that matters most in acting is now.

Action is the only thing that produces results.

Future generations will be our judge. And what we do now, as active and engaged citizens, or the opposite, will determine their verdict on us.

****

www.ingramcontent.com/pod-product-compliance
Lightning Source LLC
Chambersburg PA
CBHW070825260726
48660CB00005B/1987